I0080873

All poems by Samantha Underhill © 2022
Printed with permission. All rights reserved

Cover art designed by Samantha Underhill & Broken Keys Publishing © 2022
Cover Model: Samantha Underhill

Published March 2022
First Printing

No part of this book may be used or reproduced, scanned, distributed in any printed or electronic form in any manner whatsoever without the prior written permission except in the case of brief quotations embodied in reviews.

Published by Broken Keys Publishing
brokenkeypublishing@gmail.com

ISBN: 978-1-988253-36-7 (print edition)
ISBN: 978-1-988253-35-0 (digital)

Foreword

by Jonathan Maberry

That Siren Call…
An Introduction

Poetry is magic.

Always has been.

It conjures images with so few words that it gently coerces the imagination of the reader –or listener—to fill in the blanks. This co-creative process allows a poem to be infinitely elastic. Although there is sometimes an intended meaning, the reader has liberty to veer away and make it uniquely their own.

Poetry is shareable magic. Whether it's an old ballad of heraldic adventure, a song picked out by a singer with a guitar, a classic work by one of the greats that entertains and informs, a piece of experimental verse scrawled on a wall or a painter's canvas, lyrics to a hip-hop diatribe, or a small set of couplets sweet enough to pull sunlight through an overcast sky, poetry connects us with magic. The ability of the poet to speak the language of understanding through imagery, motif, metaphor or other device rather through explicit description is staggering. So few words to say so much.

I'm a novelist. I write very long books in various genres, and some of these clock in somewhere north of 150 thousand words. Hell, my shortest novel is 85 thousand words. I also write comic books and scads of short stories. In prose works like these I have all those words to set a scene, describe action, craft characters, weave interactions, and tell my story.

Some poets can do about as much in a dozen lines of verse.

That is sorcery to me.

It's one of many reasons why I begin each writing day by reading poetry aloud. The efficient lyricism helps me get to the heart of whatever it is I want to say or describe without carrying more weight of words than that image or scene needs. It actually allows me to write long novels while keeping the metaphors, the figurative and descriptive language, the pace and voice, and the other elements of the prose writer's craft as smooth, tight, and enjoyable as possible. I doubt my writing would be as good or as popular if I did not read poetry every day.

In fact, I know that. I can feel when the essence of poetic thought whispers in my ear in a voice that enchants me and guides me.

Which brings me to this collection.

Poet Samantha Underhill writes poetry about some of the things I feature in my novels. Strange creatures, ancient gods, intense emotions, complex psychology, myths and legends. I was drawn to her poetry because with any given piece there are visible layers. You can read a poem one day and then on another day, or in another mood, read it again and there has been a magical transformation. The meaning of the poem has changed.

Poetry is like that. It is often less about the mood of the poet when composing than that of the reader in the moment of experiencing. A poem might be very dark and bitter in one reading, and then lighter and more amusedly sarcastic when read again. Another piece might appear to be about one thing, but – having become familiar with its thematic veneer—on closer inspection it tells a different story. Or a different version of the same story.

The very best poems are those that can be, on one hand, old friends whose flow is a joy to read aloud; and on the other hand becomes entirely new when read after some time and personal growth has happened.

Magic.

One enchanting element that speaks to me is the motif of the 'siren'. To those who don't know the folkloric and mythological backstory of these creatures they seem to be synonymous with an irresistible romantic attraction. And yet the sirens were not at all what they appeared to be. To the student of history and literature, the siren is a monster who uses a plaintive call to lure sailors to their deaths. They are very much like mermaids of the pre-Disney world –creatures of unparalleled beauty who enticed seafarers with a promise of passion and ecstasy but then reveal their true natures as hideous and carnivorous beasts. Many vampire stories have the same structure, with the vampire using some kind of glamor –in the magical sense of that word-- to appear beautiful or handsome and then when the trap is sprung the tearing fangs come out.

Samantha Underhill's poems have the same glamor, and they call with the same compelling voices. They are beautiful to look at and read, but there are dangers there. These poems bite.   They draw blood.

As they should.

Some can make you cry because beneath the surface is visible heartbreak –old and new. Though, if you are hesitant about shedding tears you probably shouldn't be reading any kind of verse beyond greeting cards. Though…if you've bought this book then I seriously doubt that's the case.

So, there is much to decode in these poems that make up Sadness of the Siren. I suggest that you read them once, consider. Then take a breath, read them again.

Go deeper.

Peel it back, layer by layer and catch the subtle fragrance of new meanings. Not just those the writer subtly intended, but based on your own changeable moods.

Start at the beginning, the middle, the end. Read in or out of order. Go wherever the siren's call takes you.

Embrace this magic.

Enjoy!

-Jonathan Maberry
San Diego, California, January 2022

Dedication

The book of poetry is dedicated to all those friends, family, and colleagues who encouraged me to find my own paths and understand my value. To those who don't always understand why I have to do things the way I do, but support me anyway. To the loveliest online community on this planet, who possibly support me emotionally more than any group of people ever have. To my family who put up with my insanity and need for creative outlet and time. To Broken Keys Publishing, who helped me overcome my fears of releasing these works. To my dear mother and my recently passed father, for always believing I was the best at everything.

As wrong as I thought they were, maybe I shine now and again. And finally to the readers, I hope my light shines to you in the darkness. Find hope. You're never truly alone.

I. Aptera, or Sadness of the Siren

Persephone, my friend and companion,
Stolen by Hades, taken deep into his canyon

Demeter, in her fury and in her rage
Added to me wings but put me in a cage

To live only by the will of those
Who made me a demon, as they chose

Forced to draw in, but never to possess
The affections of those attempting access

It's my siren song that draws them near
These oceans of people from everywhere

But if too close they come to pass
The gates of my heart they then bypass

Then rueful murder I must sadly commit
Should I determine to live, their throats must slit

A demon says those on the outside looking in
A tortured soul says I who sits without control within

Smiling in beauty, the muses they suggest
A competition of song to their grand talent attest

The challenge, oh, my heart is not in it
I determine, by choice, that I shall not win it

And so, my feathers, from the root they are plucked
By the muses a crown made, unsportsmanlike conduct

And in both woeful loss and happiness of end
Pale I turn, into Aptera I am rend

II. Song of Death

Enchanted siren, in your meadow, starred with infinite soft flowers,

Why sing you, your luring songs, for the sailors all the hours?

Is a home within the Sirenuse on Anthemusa not enough —

To fulfill your lusts for harmony? Must you be so rough?

Dragging down the sailor's soul to a regimented damnation —

Hades ruling, winsome, triumphant - for each and every occasion?

Must men take extremes to avoid their gruesome fate?

Tie them to a mast, plug their ears, in a helpless state?

Does an evil smirk spread slowly across your lovely face —

When you see them make attempts to leave you wholly unscathed?

Is this your choice to torture them so —
or perhaps it's your condemnation?

Cursed to be the teasing lure, unable to have cessation,

Of this madness, your own accursed voice —
your beauty and your hellfire?

Internal, you are a tormented soul —
hating the duty for which you are required

But without choice, sadly you sing, and dream of a deathless day.

Hope lost, song of death, ringing throughout the bay.

III. The Unanswered Plea

Gods above or Gods below
Grace and mercy upon me bestow
Hear my prayer, my need, my plea
Pity have on a lowly soul like me

Desire and hope for another's love
A beauteous rare gift sent from above
You are great where I am small
I beg of you, on my knees, I crawl

To thy power, To thy will
Obeying your commands ever still
All these years, I have yielded
Under your authority have I been shielded

But loveless and filled with fear am I
Yearning for fondness to be drawing nigh
Desiring love but never fully granted
Obedience and duty leaving disenchanted

Imploring, entreating for a moment's happiness
Again, I wail, pleading for one single chance
For thy favor, beseeching thy pity
For understanding of my weak humanity

Internal, my spirit, it miserably sobs
External, I continue devotedly my jobs
Without protest, as I am but a speck
In the dust of the stars that the skies bedeck

IV. Dark Beauty

Darkness and light
Beauty and shade
These combinations
Are not easily made

> Yet there are lively beings
> Who are magnetically drawn
> To the deep ocean and midnight
> Misunderstood - woebegone

Unaccepted by either side
The darkness nor the light
A curiosity to others
Bright in love with night

> But such an adoration
> Isn't truly that curious
> For much beauty is fathomless
> This love is not that mysterious

Hidden and shrouded
The elegance of the icy moon
More than meets the eye
Not all is damnation and gloom

> For in the darkest immeasurable deeps
> Exists the perfect space
> For a bright bubbly individual
> To glow and show her grace

The contrast of the light
Against the blackness, stark
Reveals the infinite love
Growing within her heart

> So do not shun the one
> Who does not seem to fit
> Their adoration is deeper
> Than any other writ

V. Sirens of Night

In the deeply dangerous forest
    With lightning flash, the song begins
        Thunder, chirping, scuttling
            Branches pulsating in the winds

                Owls that screech and hoot
                like Sirens in the night
            Calling all deeper into the woods
            although it is bereft of light

Leaf and insect covered trails
    Barely visible underfoot
        Weaving throughout the trees
            With minimal light output

                Cracking the undergrowth
                With each and every step
            Adds to this music of the night
            Soul catching, heart upswept

Fragrances only heightening
    The irresistible summons of the evening
        Earthy fungi, scent of pine
            Almost leaves you reeling

                What is that call, that cry, that howl
                Ringing throughout the air?
            Is it a crow's caw? A wolf's howl?
            Perhaps a haunt is there.

And where are you headed
    On this unexpected excursion?
        Forget all reason, abandon agenda
            Into the darkness, complete immersion

VI. Savage Fire

In the dusk of evening,
Hear the ringing call
'Cross hill, valley, and heather
Beckoning, "come one, come all"

Deep into the nocturnal forest
These sirens bid you come
To join in the woodland chorus
To feel the beat of the drum

The flames wildly are dancing
In the bonfire lit tonight
Wondrous women, freely prancing
Care and woe out of sight

Form a circle all around
The licking fire and smoke
Ancient rituals infinitely profound
Bodies communicating, words unspoke

The shadows against the woods
Seem to form a never-ending ring
Of bodies, no, souls, like gods
Merging, motion, a voice that sings

The flicker luminous against the skin
Dances and leaps on the external
Reflecting the blissful joy felt within
Angelic, elevated, ethereal, supernal

But who is this that sits in the dark of night?
An uninvited visitor, kneeling just out of sight?

Is it a spector, a ghoul, or some woodland creature
Or perhaps some shy fool too scared to be featured

To join in the dance, to feel the exhilaration?
Perhaps the draw to simply watch is too strong a temptation.

VII. Night Goddess

Immortal, oh goddess of night,
Moon and starshine gleam at thy delight
Darkness dispelled with a wave of your hand
Gracefully spanning, the cosmos command

But alone you abide in the night sky
At times I believe I hear you softly sigh
While igniting the fires in every constellation
The flames within extinguished without flirtation

Are you lonely, oh brilliance, in the dark?
Is there someone, somewhere who makes your heart spark?
Or is solitude your wish and your requirement?
Perhaps you know not your beauty and your allurement?

Lovers willing and ready to be your one and only
To treat you with care and passion forever openly
So the others might see you treasured and cared for
Respected, worshipped, as the goddess adored

Nevertheless, you shine, resplendent, radiant, oh Night
Carrying out your duties with seemingly endless delight
And pride in the mystifying art your hands create

Which warms all our souls, our hearts captivate

VIII. Irresistible Cry

The alluring seduction and tantalizing cry of the siren
With uncontrollable urge calling all of the brethren

The song of darkness that compels men to leap headfirst
Into the unknown blackness of the accursed

No more to see the day, No more to see the night
No more to fall deep in love with beauties at first sight

And what enticing words must this song contain?
What overpowering lyrics must be in this refrain?

Phrases that ignite passion and remove a man's freewill
Must certainly be complex and weave the soul with skill

But quite simple are the words that are sung to these
The melody that moves and carries along the ocean breeze,

"You matter. Your thoughts are sweet and special to me.
Come to me, know me, love me, and together we can be free."

But a caged bird cannot offer such things so freely
Thus, the man and the siren must suffer a doomed love untimely.

IX. Ill-fated Lure

Winged maids, daughters of the Earth!
Beauty personified, filled with mirth.
Purity appears to drip from every pore.
But hostility and chaos lives within your core.

Mortal man simply cannot resist.
On this fact your wildness persists.
Capable of captivating every audience.
Luring them in with no pain of conscience.

Beguiler, seductress, seducer, vamp
Are there any who can escape your camp?
Should one escape would you be glad or terrified
Or perhaps at possible loss of power, petrified?

Would your broken hubris, greed, and pride
Break you down, shattered, deep inside?
Would you drown in your flood of tears
After one loss over all these years?

Perhaps the survival of man would bring joy?
Your desire stronger to love than to destroy.
But a murderous wretch, you have been labeled,
In each and every story and fable.

It may be that one cannot truly know
Without first being drawn in by you so?
Our curiosity may never be satiated
Unless to you, being drawn, we are fated.

X. Longing without End

Longing
is a whisper

Longing
is the wind

Longing
is the hurricane of unexpected feelings that stir within

Like the winds of a tornado, swirling around the soul

Longing is a question without an answer or reached goal

Longing
is a need

Longing
is a prayer

Longing
is the desire to have someone to be there

Humming a siren's song helps brings love ever closer

But ending in sadness and death, not greater closure

Longing
is a pit

Longing
is the ocean

Longing
is the unrelenting waves of the great deep sea

Dashing hopes but stirring feelings that continue to grow the craving
inside

Longing is the crying for another until no more tears will fill the eyes

XI. Earth and Ocean

My love is rooted with his feet firmly on the ground
A great tree with strong branches spreading all around

His attributes and qualities represented in each little leaf
But our differences, too great, will from us, love thieve

For I am The Siren, bound to the rocks of the ocean
Bent to the will and movement of the sea's constant motion

Which over me forever has all reign and all power
Its requirements and its responsibilities my soul devour

Can a fish love a man?
Would that fit into God's omnipotent plan?

Heavens no, there is no place for us!
No time set aside for such a love, thus

We must move on and accept our assigned responsibility
Dutifully, and with the expected grace and humility

So weep, my love, for the loss of what cannot be
And dream for a day when our hearts together will weave

XII. Yearning

No light among the heavens
Can match the luminescence in your eyes
The hope and expectation
Of future connections arise

Visualizations of things that could be
But unfortunately, not that are
Leaving me sorely yearning
Wanting, needing from afar

Wishes for close whispers
Light touches on the neck
Hungry for the trembling breath
Felt across my back

Need for the nearness of you
The gift of your inspiration
Infatuation is exceeded
Required close perspiration

Under the spell you've cast
Happily obsessing
Given the opportunity
Would have no difficulty expressing

The depth of the feeling
that flows inside my veins
Melting the blood within
Distance holding the chains

That keep us separated –

Yearning.

XIII. The Draw

The curve of her lips
Matches her hips
That gleam and the glint in her eye

The melody that flows
Out of her mouth grows
Fills heart gaps and makes me sigh

Her seductive Siren song
Within the soul does throng
Luring me - knowing I may die

But what a death is this
To momentarily feel such bliss
I did not know anything so high

A minute, an hour, a second
Her call to me - her beckon
Would all be well worthwhile

For this brief interlude
Would provide a new view
And my death - at least in style

XIV. Charming, Not Sincere

I did not ask to be the Siren
It was a role I was given
Never once was I aspiring
Or soul-consuming driven

I did not ask to be the Siren
Raised to be simply charming
Insincerity in my wiring
Assigned to do more harming

I did not ask to be the Siren
Without a chance for love
Although my heart is firing
Relationships not sent from above

I did not ask to be the Siren
Just wanted to be human
Luring souls is simply tiring
This lifestyle is subhuman

I did not ask to be the Siren
Pulling loved ones to hell
I would rather be expiring
My soul in Hades dwell

I did not ask to be the Siren
Convincing others of fake desire
But this role I am acquiring
Must accept hosting the Lake of Fire

XV. Death is No End

Weeping will not bring me back
Nor should it do so
Because I never truly left
My love within you grows

I am the warmth in your socks
When your feet are cold
I am the gasping in your laughter
When the giggles overflow

The thunder you adore
and the storms that bring the rain
That help you to sleep better
And get you through this pain

The stories and imagination
You inherited them from me
Will spread out forevermore
For other generations to see

Because I know you'll share them
Your heart and mine will meld
Through your carrying forward
The history we have upheld

And while I know you'll weep
Just be sure that that's not all
One day you will join me
At the time you get the call

Then once you're here
Oh, you will truly see
How you reflect within the stars
For your friends and family

XVI. Thunderous Sighs

As quiet as they are
Your sighs are thunderous
So soft that they are loud
As slowly they pull from under us

Any semblance of connection
Of our original intentions
Altered from life changes
Moving to increasing tensions

Encircling birds, we, seek a landing
But finding only an unforgiving ocean
Separating the two once conjoined
Going through the motions

Are wounds so deep
That they cannot be mended?
Is it all so broken
That forgiveness cannot be extended?

Goodness no! Fragments may reconnect
When a lovelight still embers
Within not just one, but the two
The good of the past, the soul remembers

As the warm memories unfold,
Hot passions are reignited
Palms sweat, heart skip beats,
Leaving each other breathless and excited

Now sighs so thunderous
From loving with such feeling
Orgasmic connection
Leaving all reeling.

XVII. Without Kindness

How is the world with so much misery replete?
People everywhere, simply filled with conceit.
Is kindness that difficult to offer to one another?
Helpful words hardly shared among brothers.

Of the human race is sweetness so unusual?
Preference leaning toward the cruel and the critical.
Jaded and cynical. Bitter and spaded.
A disparaging world that we have all created.

Depression and unhappiness, our babies we birth.
Making it quite difficult to want to live on this earth.
But with a bit of effort and leaning toward nice.
Perhaps this mistake we will not commit twice.

So this day, right now, do not wait a minute longer.
Go out and compliment someone, make them feel stronger.
Show them the colors you see from your eyes.
Reveal to them that their internal beauty shines.

And perhaps you'll find that they compliment you too -
Making you feel elation that you never really knew.
So, with newfound energy and validated purpose -
You will help others, yourself no longer feel hopeless.

XVIII. Is There No Hope?

There are times when no hope seems present and accounted for
Times when basic tasks and activities plummet to the floor
When no particular pathway emerges above the rest
Because one is so tired and worn from attempting to do best

When endeavor and effort have never truly succeeded
You're only older, not wiser, no matter how you pleaded
"Is there no hope," that is the question you will ask
Robotic motions, carrying out all of the mundane tasks

You begin to seek miracles, as you never have before
An alteration of direction, to improve your current score
When horror and anguish have settled as your daily norm
Is there any way out of this disastrously deep dark storm?

But all at once, a flash, a bolt, of something unexpected!
Suddenly appears out of the blue, starts in your direction!

Your heart and soul are curiously stirred with new excitement!
What is this hope, this inexplicable feeling of connection?

Surely some consequential, extraordinary, significant occurrence
Has created these foreign feelings,
responsible for their appearance

Yet as you seek to find the owner of this change so astounding
This cause for hope is simple - a smile - within you is resounding

XIX. The Coming Light

There is light shining within the darkness
There is a destination at the end of the path
There is meaning among the madness
There is a hope in the terrible aftermath

It's an opportunity to let someone in
Which may seem daunting and frightful
And difficult to find where to begin
But the outcomes can be simply delightful

Association, connection, bonds, and ties
In the darkest corners, its together we rise

So, do not isolate, do not detach
Seclusion does not help to attach

Seek others like you - you are not very alone
There are common problems to which we're all prone

And to those who currently are not sinking
Remember when walking and rising were almost too hard
Recall those times when there was no right thinking
When everything you did seemed marred

Offer to be a helping hand to all those around you
Be the coming light to those in darkness
Show them the brain lies are not true
Give them warmth where once was starkness

The Coming Light is you.

XX. Umbra

Shade and shadow
Stygian

Dark beauty bestow
Crepuscule

When twilight ensues
Gloaming

The darkness consumes
Tenebrous

Confined from outside light
Obscured

Swallowed in deep night
Opacous

Growing ally profound
Resonant

Devoured by abyss drowned
Bottomless

Immeasurable horrors await
Engrossed

Self-awareness dissipates
Exhaustion

Dominion is welcomed
Release

Desire to be numb
Relinquish

Overpowered but free

Shades of umbra are all I see

XXI. Madness of New Love

The madness of love is an unquenchable thirst

An intensity of need that is ever-growing
Insatiable hunger, maddening desire
The rush of heat warms cheeks to glowing

The madness of love is a newly active volcano

Fiery feelings rising and threatening to burst
A wild stirring within that tingles all internal
The magma inside molten from the hungry thirst

The madness of love is dawn of ardent infatuation

Swirling pining thoughts, pulse begins to race.
Feelings building, swelling, threatening to peak
Desire blooming each time you see their face

The madness of love is a never-ending ache

Impassioned need and irrational jealousy
Imagination enlivened by a mere soft touch
Lighting the flame, needing them desperately

The madness of love is yielding to a siren song

Anything they say will beckon you to their call
Pledging yourself to them wholly and spiritually
No matter what future it is that you may befall

XXII. Beauty in Repose

My love he lies upon the bed we share
His body partially obscured by the sheets
Between which our souls we bare
When our bodies merge complete

Our lips, tongues, full bodies convening
Sharing stories our voices cannot speak
Giving our pining hunger its meaning
Urgent pleasures bringing us to peak

In those moments after these conversations
No part of the interaction needing amendment
Sighing softly, body shivering sensations
There he sweetly lies in utter contentment

It's in that hour his beauty overwhelms me how
The contours of his form, his lightly parting lips
Relaxation of his normally furrowed brow
The spreading of his muscular legs and hips

The light streaming into the room, illuminates his skin
Highlighting his jaw, eye lashes, the shape of his nose
It beckons me, urges me, to touch his manly form again
But for now, I refrain, and view his beauty in repose

He blissfully moans so lightly without intention
Breathes my name, sweetly falling from his mouth
At this word, that pure loving mention
No longer contained, my lips move south

To begin anew our love's communication
The language that only our bodies can utter
Eyes meeting in renewed loving flirtation
As mouths move and melt like warm butter

XXIII. Come Be My Siren

Come be my deadly siren
Use me briefly for thy score
Take me to the deep abyss
Drowning, but still begging for more

Envelop me with thy magic
Yearning for greater show of thy powers
Let me ink my adoration on thy scales
Death coming, but pleasure for hours

The feathers of thy expansive wings
Enfold me against thy agile body
Charm me, lure me, fall in temptation
Of you there is no equal or copy

Thy silken hair surrounds my chest
As seductively you move to reveal
The expanse of thy hips and thy breasts
No longer by thy lovely locks concealed

Arouse me with thy rosy lips
Thy voice, thy song, thy lies
Momentary celestial pleasure
And in happy death, I die

XXIV. Calling Aphrodite

Oh, beguiling enchantress, seducer, mistress
Barriers down, you will find me resistless
O, Divine Aphrodite, how dare I upon you call?
Magnetically to you I am hypnotically drawn

Artful strategy of lustful schemes
Flow easily from your reddened lips
Into your eyes, I am delivered into dreams
Lusting for the curve of your hips

I pray you come to me once if once only
Love's anguish has left me deeply lonely
Filled with bewildered, hopeless desire
Only your touch can quench this blazing fire

But this day you flee from my hopeful love
While tomorrow you will eagerly pursue
Wooing notes sent from heaven above
Find me not unwilling! Let our love ensue!

XXV. Moon Goddess, Hear My Cry!

Pleading prayers, I shout at the Night sky
"I beg of you, do not ignore me, hear my cry!"
But the Moon Goddess seems to never reply

But hark! Slowly the glow of the moon seems to turn my way
"Moon, I pray, please hear what I have to say!"

"Small, dear one," the Moon speaks, *"so fervently you have called,
Please share the concern that has you so enthralled."*

"Moon," says I, in a meek voice rather frail and dim
"Why is love so difficult, its outcome always so grim?

"Love is meant to warm, to heal, and feed the very soul."
"So why is it over me that melancholy overflows?"

"Love escapes the grasp of forever.
It seems, where it is, I am concerned.
Will I never be granted it fully ever
For keeps, as I have always yearned?"

The Moon, she smiles, but in a sorrowful fashion.
*"Little darling one, you must understand,
love is never owned. It is a shared passion
that does not appear on command...*

*"...Love an experience for which all the people clamor
And pray for but remember love is only ever loaned...*

*"...but do not weep, my tiny, cherished petite one.
For while love may be brief, its effects are felt
Across a lifetime, warmth, like neverending sun
And though tears may fall, be happy with what you're dealt...*

*"It is those who have loved who are the most fortunate.
For those who have not, greatly suffer disproportionate.
Your grief and loss and your tear-stained eyes
Are only proof of the love your heart forevermore supplies."*

XXVI. Closeness

Dream

All within my mind
Never actually together, always apart
Holding me tenderly, your soft touch

Gleam

No word, no rhyme
Need for your body, sensual art
Could describe the desire I feel such

Steam

From our climb
Future together, never ever to part
Climax at a distance, always in touch

Scream

Desperate for time
Separated by circumstance, holding heart
Closeness, feeling you, needing you so much

XXVII. Frozen

Slowly dying within myself
Bereft of feeling and light
Returning the books back to the shelf
Never reading them, not quite

Never convincing the brain to process
Had only stared at the words
Dwelling on the negative and the stress
Thoughts flitting around like birds

Focus lost to icy feelings
Internal, deeply rooted
Matters of the heart leave me reeling
Love too soft, simply muted

Requited emotions not allowed
For monsters, freaks, and failures
Sadly, slip back into the crowd
Dreaming of something pure

Heart is frozen
Put on ice
When will it be melted?

Perhaps one day to be chosen
Without a price
Nothing more regretted

XXVIII. Without You

Thoughts, but no direction
Oceans, but no breeze
Color, but no variety
Forests, but no trees
Sustenance, but no flavor
Existence without ease

Daily tasks now move too slow
Each day that you've been gone
My doubt and anxiousness overflow
Feeling more inward drawn

You gave me a love I had not known
Its presence caring, raw
If only I had realized how time had flown
More tightly would I claw

To dig my nails deeper to keep you near
Not let you slip so softly away
But my desire only won't keep you here
No matter how hard I pray

What drew you away, I do not understand
We were still very much in love
Clinging firmly to one another's hands
"Us" seemed sent from Heaven above

But the day came that I had dread
You asked to explain to me
No longer should we share love's bed
You needed to be free

So now I must live without true love
I must move steadily forward
Where the heart was once, a void
The abyss that I'm drawn toward

Thoughts, but no direction
Oceans, but no breeze
Color, but no variety
Forests, but no trees
Sustenance, but no flavor
Existence without ease

XXIX. Strange

Grace and splendor in her face
Viewed and adored by all the people
But inward beauty, woven laced
Lies dormant and asleep 'til

Someone understanding of strange beauty
Sees things invisible to earthbound eyes
Beyond her looks, internal brooding
Is a nebula of celestial prize

Engulfing constellations unexplored
Ethereal abysses dark to opposing sun
Adorned internal, this wildly weird
Fierce, striking, fair one

Magnificence like this is rarely seen
Sights this beauteous, unsurpassed
Colors swirl, purple, blue, and green
Mystery of her, spell cast

Leaving the viewer breathless, awed
Gloriously bathed in her light
Although outward dark, flawed
She appears to those with natural sight

XXX. Pointing Fingers

Who is really the monster
On this dark path I've taken?
Danger in soft beauty
The soul within men awaken.

The dangerous cunning Siren
You say is evil incarnate.
But who made us this way
Will the creator not own it?

Chained to terrible duty
Never wanted to be tasked
To lure others to peril
Not once ever asked

How should I survive
Or flourish in such a place?
On this rocky coast of shipwrecks
This vile cursed space?

Binder, entangler
Charming man and winds
Enticing nearby sailors
To gruesome deathly ends

Did eloquent mother Calliope or
our absent father Achelous
Stop Demeter from cursing us
From this fate so perilous?

No! Not at all!
Simply left us to this fate -
For failing our beloved Persephone
Arriving a bit too late.

Is this murderous appointment
Deserved for our failing thus?
Our life or theirs the choice
Daily made, no positive or plus.

Orpheus, please play your lyre
Drown out our fatal voices
With your more beautiful music
Stop the demise, outside of our choices

But like a moth drawn to the flame
Our nature stained by this calling
The fire within our veins seeks
Succumbing to our enthralling

We will overcome you if we can
The duality in our souls
Desiring life, desiring death
Help! It is outside our control

So, my love, man with interest
Run, don't walk, quickly flee
Plug your ears and tie to the mast
Get thee far away from me

Love is not allowed, is not meant
No lust have I, your blood to stain
My aching broken doomed heart
From me, please daily refrain

Not meant for things expected for others
Only to serve this call
Simply waiting for the end
Ready to damnation fall

But is Hellfire all that worse
Than my current situation
Hurting others, in continued curse
Praying, hoping, seeking salvation

XXXI. Demon

Is the Siren just a monster not deserving of real life?
Is she a creature of darkness not worthy of any light?

Loving and hating everything at once
Dual personality, out of equal balance

Pain - the only constant companion
Kindness never given, never won

Scores of people I have lost
Love and friendship too high a cost

Given this fate so definedly twisted
Never to love, a life unassisted

So distant from the place I had hoped to be
Fate sealed by past choices
Heart-shattered, unloved eternally

In torment, I pine, burning, misunderstood
The others see evil selfish tendencies
No capability of happiness or of good
No exceeding limits, no transcendencies

When seen immediately I am adored
or I am emphatically feared
While lovers see external beauty
Accusers see blood smeared

On the hem of my garment
And look into my eyes,
shouting, "Monster! Demon!"
Running away, no surprise.

Hearing their cries, I think to myself,
"Am I or am I not?
What is it that I prize
Is bloodshed what I want?"

Losing my hold on reality
"What do I feel? What am I made to think?"
Slipping further, deeper into the abyss
Within myself, increasingly sink

"Can a Siren drown, I wonder?"
Perhaps that is the end I seek.

Droning words, regularly heard
Fill up the spaces in my mind
"Demon!" the small, simple word,
suffocates and makes me blind

XXXII. Broken Wings

These wings of mine are plucked and clipped
Unfit to take any flight
From me this freedom was wholly ripped
By my lack of thought and foresight

Decisions made, trust given
Too swiftly for good measure
Forced into a path, evil driven
Forever lacking true pleasure

Or so I thought but suddenly
A hand drops to hold mine
Lifting me from off the ground
Gazing at me from eyes that shine

I notice his many painful scars,
and the darkness in his face
But something deeper in him warms me
Fills me with hope unerased

Lifting my hand to touch his cheek
He winces, and softly groans
Hurt, within, pain and tears overflow
"Safe," I weakly whisper, and quietly moan.

His eyes, deflecting my staring gaze
Return to me their longing
"Pain," says I, "I know too well"
Again "safe," I whisper, prolonging

Our bond and touch, I am enchanted
The first in unending ages
A rush of love I am granted
Is this freedom from our cages?

Why, I wonder, is he not injured
by my Siren song?
Fate, washed away, am I cured?
What I've hoped for, for so long?

Or is it he who is special?
What is this common connection?
Is he also demon or a devil
Capable of showing affection?

Decidedly, I wash my mind
Determined it does not matter
Quickly I compliment him
Turning on charm and flatter

A smile spreads softly across his face,
"I am yours, and You are mine.
No need for luring, no need for tricks
Your broken wings, together we will fix."

Then fly together
Far away
from all the pain and strife
Finally as one with hope for happy life.

About the Author

Samantha Underhill is a poet, voice artist, educator, researcher, mother, and lover of all things dark but beautiful.

Born in Appalachia, Samantha's connection to haunting, soul-touching scenery, music, and folklore, gives her a unique connection to deep meaningful melancholy.

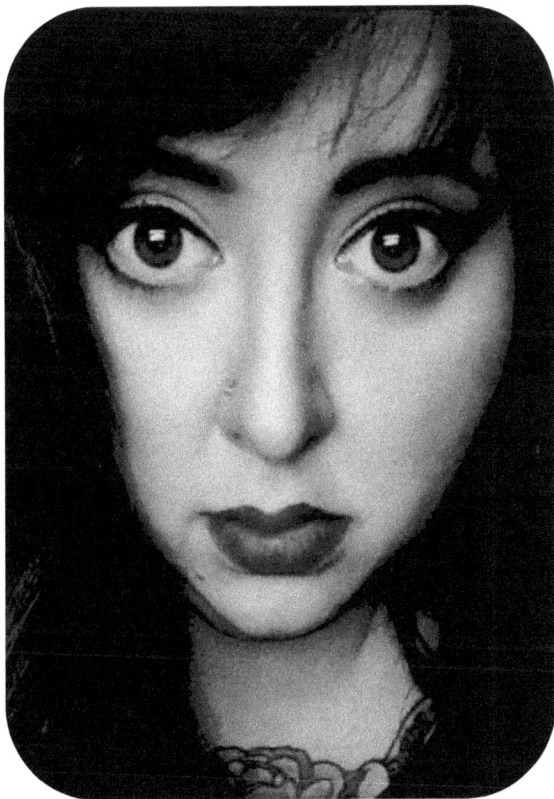

Samantha is influenced by writers of dark storytelling poetry and literature, such as H.P. Lovecraft, Edgar Allan Poe, and Jorge Luis Borges.

It can be said that Samantha lives in duality. Her bright bubbly uplifting personality often contrasts the unexpected storms within. Those who know her, love her for both.

Follow more of her artistry by scanning the code to the right with your smart device camera.

SCAN ME

About the Publisher

Broken Keys Publishing has won the 2021 CPACT-NCR Best Publishing Company Award, 2020-22 Faces of Ottawa Award for Best Publisher, Faces of Ottawa 2021 Book of the Year Award (for Thin Places: The Ottawan Anthology), Faces of Ottawa 2022 Book of the Year Award (for Love & Catastrophē Poetrē) & nominated for the CPACT-NCR 2019 Small Business Excellence Award.

About the Book Covers

The front cover of this book is an artistic rendering of the poet, designed by the author, Samantha Underhill. The author desired to show the longing and melancholy within herself – mimicking the emotions of her poetry.

The back cover uses a public domain image of John William Waterhouse's *The Siren*, c. 1900. In *The Siren*, a survivor of shipwreck is depicted clinging for life to a rock as a young siren lures him with music from her abalone shell harp. John William Waterhouse created a series of oil and pencil art of mermaids and sirens. Waterhouse was said to be attracted to sirens as females who had power in beauty and represented feminine danger. The original image is shared in public domain by Sotheby's (Lot. 12) and currently resides in private collection.

Also available from Broken Keys Publishing

Symphonies of Horror:
Inspirational Tales by H. P. Lovecraft: The Symbiot Appendum

Thin Places: The Ottawan Anthology
(Winner of the Faces of Ottawa 2021 Book of the Year Award)

Love & Catastrophé Poetré
(Winner of the Faces of Ottawa 2022 Book of the Year Award)

Ghosts and Other Chthonic Macabres
(Winner of the Faces of Ottawa 2023 Book of the Year Award)

Missing the Exit, *by Michael Adubato*

Little Dragon, *by Jana Begovic*
Poisonous Whispers, *by Jana Begovic*
Mishko the Friendly Bat, *by Jana Begovic*

Kat and the Meanies, *by Anna Blauveldt*
The Leavetaking, *by Anna Blauveldt*
A Plum Hollow Coven Story: Awakening, *by Anna Blauveldt*

Lost Americana: The End of the American Dream,
by Scott Cravens

A Time for All Seasons, *by Sharleen A. McCorrister*
The Death Whisperer, *by Sharleen A. McCorrister*

Clean Water for Lukong, *by Pat Moore*

Troubled Waters, *by Mike Sadava*

Under a Maple Tree, *by Jagjeet Sharma*
Measure of a Wo/man, *by Jagjeet Sharma*

Titles by Allysina Shinestone:
Mad Monks and Blood Diamonds
Circumstantial Encounters
Masked Intentions
Gathering Fragments
The Forgotten Fear
Entranced Entanglement

Love Defined: Discover God's Love for You, *by Nancy Steele*

Sadness of the Siren, *by Samantha Underhill*

Titles by Michel Weatherall:
The Symbiot 30th Anniversary: The Nadia Edition
Necropolis 10th Anniversary, The Alia Moubayed Edition
The Refuse Chronicles
The Symbiot Trilogy Box-Set
Ngaro's Sojourney
A Dark Corner of My Soul
Down Darkened Corridors

The Brain Colour and Learning Book, Vol. 1,
Le Cerveau - livre de coloriage et apprentissage: volume 1
by Maria Zamfir, PhD & Marion Van Horn, PhD

www.brokenkeyspublishing.com

Broken Keys
Publishing
&
PRESS
Ottawa, Ontario, Canada

www.ingramcontent.com/pod-product-compliance
Lightning Source LLC
LaVergne TN
LVHW052037080426

835513LV00018B/2366